Walt Disney

LIVING DESERT

A True-Life Adventure

ADAPTED FOR SCHOOL USE BY JANE WERNER WATSON

ILLUSTRATED WITH COLOR PHOTOGRAPHS

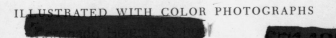

THE L. W. SINGER COMPANY, INC · SYRACUSE, NEW YORK

DISTRIBUTED IN CANADA BY J. M. DENT & SONS (CANADA), LIMITED

Strange and beautiful plants adapt themselves to the dry desert.

What is a Desert?

A desert is a place where there are plains without grass, mountains without trees, strange plants without leaves. It is a place where so little rain falls that most plants and animals cannot live. The sun shines hotly almost every day. But hot sunshine is not what makes a desert. Lack of rain is the cause. And why does so little rain fall?

Rain is brought by winds which are blowing most of the time. The oceans from which the winds draw water cover more than two-thirds of the earth. It would seem that every place should get enough rain.

Wind crumbles the rocks into huge dunes of sand.

But in some places mountain ranges keep the rain winds from going over them. The winds drop their rain when they blow against the mountains. And the land beyond becomes a desert.

When the wind does reach the desert, it is dry. The dry wind works into cracks in the rocks. It crumbles some rock to sand and piles it into dunes. Other rock is carved by the wind and the blowing sand into shapes that are both beautiful and strange.

Water shapes the desert, too. When a rain does come, it falls in one wild burst. There is no soil to soak it up, nor roots to hold it back. The water runs away in a swift rushing flood that slashes through rock, carving deep canyons as it goes.

4

GREAT AMERICAN
DESERT

GOBI

GREAT ARABIAN
DESERT

SAHARA

ATACAMA

GIBSON
& VICTORIA
DESERTS

KALAHARI

Principal deserts of the world

The United States has one of the great deserts of the world. In the Far West, the Sierra Nevada and Cascade Mountains block the Pacific rain winds. To the east of these mountains, from California's Death Valley east to Texas and from Oregon south into Mexico, stretches the Great American Desert.

Great American Desert

SIERRA NEVADA MOUNTAINS

GREAT AMERICAN
DESERT

PACIFIC
OCEAN

Plants adapted to desert life

Plants of the Desert

At first glance the desert looks bare and dead. But there is plenty of life. It is not easy to live without water. But some animals and plants have learned how.

One thing desert plants must do without is broad green leaves. Most plants take in air and sunlight through their leaves. But moisture evaporates from them, too.

Desert plants cannot afford to lose moisture. So they shrivel their leaves up into needles. Or they roll them into tubes. Or they turn their leaves into thick sponges to hold water, and cover them with prickly spines. The spines keep desert animals from drinking up this water supply.

Many desert plants store water in their stems, too. They are called succulents or "juicy ones." Some stems are as round as a barrel—on the barrel cactus. Some tower like organ pipes. We call them organ pipe cacti. Some are as big as trees. One of these, the Joshua tree, is pictured on page eighteen.

There are very few real trees on the desert. The few desert willows, feathery smoke trees, and the cottonwoods are often found beside desert water holes.

But there are many shrubs—creosote bushes and round, spicy-smelling gray green sage, juniper and desert holly. So the desert is living indeed.

Sagebrush

Elf owl

Strange Bird Nests

The desert is almost without trees, yet there are birds. And the birds build nests. Where do they build? In the prickly cactus plants. Each bird, it seems, has a favorite cactus.

The mother bird chooses her cactus plant. You might think the prickly spines would frighten her away. But she catches the sharp thorns sideways in her beak and snaps them off where she wants to build her nest. She is happy to have the rest of the thorns there. They protect her and her family from their enemies, for most animals stay away from those prickly points.

8

Thrashers prefer the tree-like cholla (*choyya*) which may grow ten feet tall. The dove and cactus wren make their homes among the spoon-shaped joints of the flat-growing prickly pear cactus.

In the tall "skyscraper of the desert," the giant saguaro (*sa-wa-ro*), live the small elf owl and the swift red-tailed hawk. Its straight trunk columns may tower 30 to 50 feet high. The woodpecker pecks out his hole high above the sun-baked rock and settles down comfortably at home.

The mother cactus wren has one more trick. She builds several nests. When a hungry snake spots a tidy wren nest and slithers over to it, the chances are that it will be empty.

A roadrunner pecks at a snake

Diamond-backed rattlesnake

Rattlesnake the Hunter

A rattlesnake hunches his four-and-a-half feet of coils along the desert sand. His broad head swings from side to side. He is trying to pick up the trail of some small, tasty animal.

Above his mouth he has two scent pits. They are much more sensitive than our noses. If there is the faintest trace of an animal's body warmth left on the sand, he can pick it up. Now it is the trail of a pocket mouse he finds. So he hunches along after her.

The tiny pocket mouse (she weighs less than an ounce and is only about six inches long to the tip of her tail) knows she should not be out in the daylight. There are too many dangers about.

But she has babies at home in the snug, grass-lined sleeping room of her deep burrow. She wants to fill all the store rooms in the burrow's side tunnels with tasty seeds for them.

She is tucking seeds swiftly into her fur-lined cheek pouches. She does not see the big snake coming down her trail, but his tail rattles warn her. With one push of her paws she empties her cheek pouches. And away she streaks toward home. She uncovers a side tunnel. Down she goes and closes it behind her. Rattlesnake must find himself another meal.

Pocket mouse

Peccary versus Bobcat

It is the cool of the morning. On the edge of the desert a band of peccaries are out hunting for food. Their rough fur coats were not planned for desert sun. So they want to eat early and sleep through the heat of the day.

The peccaries are wild pigs. They have rough fur coats. Like other pigs they have good appetites. They like eggs, lizards, snakes, small animals, roots, grubs, and fruits. With all these to choose from they seldom go hungry.

The peccaries are usually peaceable. But when a baby wanders away from the band and a hungry bobcat spies him, the whole band goes to the rescue.

The bobcat, with his sharp claws, is a famous fighter. But the peccaries are twice as heavy as he. And there are a dozen or more peccaries, grunting angrily. The bobcat looks for a tree to climb. But there is only a prickly saguaro. From its top he snarls his rage at the peccaries and waits until they leave.

Ground Squirrels

It is morning on the desert. Out come the busy ground squirrels. They are always hunting food. They may carry home in their cheek pouches as many as a hundred seeds at a time. They like to eat mesquite *(mes-keet)* beans and the pea-like seeds of the palo verde *(pah-lo ver-dee)* or green stem, smoke tree, and the rest of the desert bean family. They nibble at cactus plants, too, neatly avoiding the spines. The juice gives them all the water they need.

Ground squirrels are hard workers. They climb slender stalks after seeds they cannot reach. They hollow out small hiding places under rocks to store some of their seeds.

The ground squirrels leap lightly over the ground as they go. They do not want to leave a trail their enemies can follow.

The ground squirrels never stop to play. But when a sharp alarm sounds, everyone stops work. Mothers hurry their babies down into burrows.

What is the danger? It is a Gila monster. He is a big lizard whose bite is poisonous to them.

An enemy is sighted.

The Gila monster moves on

The Gila monster is beautifully colored. His scaly coat is patterned like Indian beadwork. But the ground squirrels do not stop to admire his beauty. Most of them climb bushes or hide underground.

A few brave ones stay. They scoop up dirt with their paws and throw it at the big lizard. He snaps at them. But they are quick to run away. Then they bounce back to throw another pawful.

The monster soon has enough of this bother. He turns and wanders away.

Now down from the bushes come the ground squirrels. Up from their burrows they bring the babies. Soon they are all back at work.

The Desert Tortoise

Plod, plod. A desert tortoise is out for a walk in the sun he loves. He moves with the firm, heavy step of a very small elephant. Now and then he stops to munch berries or green cacti. He does not even look for water. He makes his own from the juicy cactus tissues. And he stores it under his shell.

Today the tortoise is not looking for food. It is his courting season. He has an eye out for a lady tortoise. He finds one soon. But as he comes near, another male tortoise appears. That means a battle!

A tortoise fights with his forepaws and a point at the front of his lower shell. He tries to hook this skid, as it is called, under the other tortoise's shell.

Each tortoise tries to tip the other over on his back. One tortoise loses. Over he goes!

If he cannot get right side up again, he will die. His legs wave. He rocks his shell and over he goes!

A battle of tortoises

Desert Night

Night on the desert is cool after the long, hot day. Then out come the creatures who do not like the sun —the elf owl, the toad, and many others.

Night on the desert is dark and secret after the bright glare of the day. Out come the timid small creatures who would not be safe in the light.

But night on the desert has its dangers, too. It has its hunters, its hungry ones. One of these is the desert toad. His bulging eyes give him a wide view of the comings and goings around him.

The desert toad

The toad's long tongue is hinged, not in back like ours, but in front. When something tasty comes along, he can flip it out swiftly, full length.

Out from beneath the sand come the poisonous scorpions. But the toad is not interested in them. He prefers a beetle or a centipede.

Scorpions

Kangaroo Rat

The tiny kangaroo rat is a night worker. She gathers seeds and carries them home in fur-lined pouches in her cheeks.

She likes to play too. She likes to visit friends. She likes to take time for a nice dust bath. The kangaroo rat does not bathe in water. She does not even drink water. What moisture she needs she makes in her body out of the dry seeds she eats. And she bathes in dust and sand.

The kangaroo rat works at night because she has so many enemies. Snakes, owls, ringtail cats and other desert creatures all like kangaroo rats to eat.

Here is an enemy now! It is a horned rattlesnake, often called a sidewinder because he loops himself sideways over the soft sand.

Small rats and mice are the sidewinder's favorite food. But he does not go out hunting them. He waits for them to come to him.

The kangaroo rat sees him before he has time to pounce. She knows how to deal with the sidewinder. She whirls about on her long hind legs and her strong, kangaroo-like tail. And she kicks sand at the snake's eyes.

Kangaroo rat, surprised by sidewinder.

21

A sidewinder's trail

The snake has no eyelids. He cannot close his eyes against the spatter of sand. Soon he gives up and loops away sideways over the desert, leaving only his strange track—and a happy kangaroo rat.

Back she goes to the business of gathering seeds. But she keeps on guard against other enemies.

The raccoon's big-eyed cousin, the ring-tailed cat, may be on the prowl. Its over-sized ears can pick up the slightest sound. The sharp-clawed, swift-diving owl may be winging past. Its eyes can peer keenly through the darkest night. Or the diamond-backed rattler may be lurking near by. Its scent pits, keener than almost any nose, can pick up the faintest trail of scent.

Both hunters and hunted must be wide-awake and keen to live through the desert night!

The ringtail cat has a long, fluffy tail circled with black rings. She is not really a cat, but her big round black eyes can see in the dark. Her ears, can pick up the slightest scurrying sounds of little desert mice and other rodents—her favorite food.

Waiting for dinner

The wasp finds a tarantula   **The battle begins**

Pepsis Wasp

The orange and black pepsis wasp is out hunting for food for her baby-to-be. And it must be a tarantula, the largest of desert spiders, with a poisonous bite.

Now a tarantula is a large, hairy spider. He is bigger than the pepsis wasp. And he has a poisonous bite.

When they meet, it is a battle to the death. The tarantula bites the pepsis wasp. But before his poison can take effect, the wasp rubs her body along the sand. It seems to heal her somehow.

The wasp seems to know that she must sting the tarantula's abdomen. She knows that only in this soft, round part of the spider's body will her poison work. She attacks from below.

24

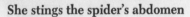

She stings the spider's abdomen   and stuffs him in a hole

She pushes her stinger again and again into the spider's body. As the poison seeps through him, he stumbles and falls.

The tarantula is not dead. But he can no longer move. That is just what the wasp wants.

She digs a hole the size of the tarantula. Some of the pebbles she drags out are as large as she is. When the hole is big enough, she drags the tarantula over and pokes him into it.

She lays one egg on the tarantula's body. Then she covers this strange nest with earth.

When the egg hatches, the baby will have enough to eat. Before it is fully grown, it will eat up all the soft parts of the tarantula.

That is the way most wasps care for their babies. They put a spider or insect of some sort into the nest for food.

Desert Storm

Dark thunderclouds come rolling over the desert. After long dry months, a desert rain is on the way.

As the thunder rumbles overhead, the desert creatures scamper for shelter. Most of them do not like rain. And this will be no gentle shower.

The clouds open. Down falls a blanket of water. A toad, who does not mind being wet, peers out into the storm, blinking his big eyes. But he cannot see much. The curtain of falling water hides the world from his sight.

As suddenly as the rain came, it stops. Out on the sun-baked desert, the water now lies in pools. Down the bare rocky hills it begins to run in streams. The streams grow as they meet in the steep-sided canyons.

Down the narrow canyons the waters rush together in a swirling flood. There is no loose soil to soak up the needed water. There is no web of roots beneath the ground to catch it and hold it back.

Away runs the precious water in a roaring flash flood. For some miles, the flood carries everything with it that it rushes over—stones, shrubs, and nests. But the sand and the dust of the desert soak up the waters at last. Soon the sun is blazing down upon the earth again.

A flash flood quickly fills the canyon.

Golden poppies cover the desert floor.

The Desert Blooms

The desert sand moves restlessly under the wind. The sun cracks open the drying ground. It is almost as if the rain had never come. But wait! The rain has done its work. All over the desert, plants were sleeping, waiting for moisture. Now, touched by the magic of the rain, they burst into bloom.

Some, like the tiny belly plants (which you have to lie flat on the ground to see), will wait ten years if necessary for the right amount of rain to come.

There are many other flowers you do not have to hunt to see. The desert is carpeted with golden poppies. The spiky ocotillo (*o-ko-teel-yo*) waves its bright flags. The short-lived cactus flowers, like those shown on the next pages, are among the loveliest of all the desert blossoms.

From bushes of blade-like leaves, the yuccas send up tall, quick-growing stalks. Soon they are aglow with pale blossoms, sometimes called "Candles of the Lord."

Even the strange, twisted arms of the Joshua tree bloom in greenish-white flowers related to the lilies.

Ocotillo

Night-blooming cereus

This is one of nature's wonders. To these plants of the desert, dwarfed and twisted by their struggle to stay alive, nature gives some of her loveliest blossoms.

No flowers in hothouse or garden can outdo the cactus blossoms for beauty of form and color. The prickly pear cactus, the pincushion, the barrel cactus, and the towering saguaro all have lovely waxy blossoms in wonderful shades.

This miraculous garden of flowers fades almost as quickly as a lovely dream. For a few short days the flowers turn the desert into a bright garden. Then the blossoms wither, and the desert is bare again.

But the blossoms have served their purpose. They have sprinkled the soil with seeds which may remain dormant until other seasons and other rains. Then they will grow and bloom in beauty again.

When the blossoms die, the desert story is not ended. For blossom time is just one part of nature's plan. Seed pods and fruit ripen in place of the blooms. They are scattered over the desert. And another season's rains will bring them, in turn, to life and flowering beauty again.

Beavertail cactus

Nature's plan is a long, large plan. It stretches
back through ages past and ahead into years to
come. Through death and birth and blossom time,
nature's desert will live on.